Y0-DJQ-191

ISBN-13: 978-1-932168-55-6
ISBN-10: 1-932168-55-9
Copyright ©2005 Veritas Press

Veritas Press, Lancaster, Pennsylvania
800-922-5082
www.VeritasPress.com

Second edition

Up in the Sky

Story by Tom Garfield

Paintings by Judith A. Hunt

Veritas Press

This book is dedicated to:

Did you ever wish you were a bird up in the sky? Larks, storks, and robins love to fly in the sky. God gave them wings. Man was not given wings, so he can not fly with the birds.

Many men did want to fly. They did want to go up in the sky and travel faster. Trips were long when you had to hike. Wilbur and Orville were brothers and they did want to fly.

They did watch the birds glide and whirl over rivers, forests, and hills. They did love God and were smart. Wilbur and Orville did work hard for a long time.

They did labor in a bike store and did fix things. Orville bent copper with a bang and a clang. Wilbur put rubber in bumpers and did fix cars.

They were alive when there were not many cars. Your grandmother was not even alive yet!

After supper they went to the shed where they began to work on big wings made of lumber and cloth. Orville and Wilbur made other, tiny wings for flying planes. They did labor for a long time.

Then, when they did tire from the work, they went to bed. When it was sunny, they did work in the yard after they left the store.

One summer morning they did take a model plane with wings to the park. Wilbur said, "Orville, let us put this plane far up in the sky!"

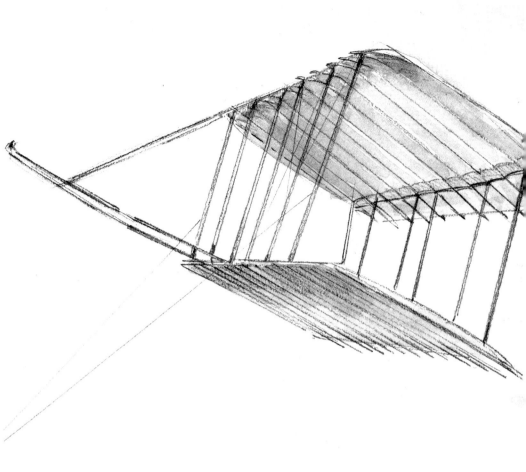

"Yes sir, it will go up far with the better wings we have put on it," said Orville. The model plane went far up with a rope on it. It did lurch and jerk in the wind up in the sky.

It did work well. The brothers were happy. They went back to the shed, and after a long time, they made a bigger plane to fly. They had many flying crafts. Some were big and some were tiny. Not all the planes did work well.

Some did crash on the grass in the park. Some had wings torn and other parts did suffer harm in the stormy wind. Wilbur and Orville did not stop wanting to make one sort of plane: a plane that was strong and big; a plane that they will ride on and fly in the sky for a long time.

Other men had been in planes, but all they did was go up and glide on the wind for a short time. The men had to hang on and ride where the wind went.

Orville and Wilbur did want to fly up and go far. They did wish to make the plane go over a hill or a river and land when and where they did pick.

Orville said, "Wilbur, we must put a motor on this plane. A motor with gas to run it. It will turn propellers on the plane to help the plane fly for a long time. The propellers will turn fast and help us get up and go far."

Wilbur said, "The motor must not be big. It must be tiny, but strong." So Wilbur and Orville did work on a motor that was tiny and strong.

They were so smart that they did it with no help. Then they put the motor on the plane and did take it to the shore.

There was lots of sand and flat land on the shore.

Orville and Wilbur got some men to help them push the plane along the flat land. Orville rode on the plane. He did start the motor. The wind was strong, but so was the plane.

"Let us go!" Orville did yell. The men did push hard and fast, and the motor did turn the propellers. With a bit of a lurch, the plane went up and did fly into the sky.

The men did watch Orville up in the sky. The plane went far with the motor thumping and humming. Orville did make the plane go back and forth.

After some time, he did land with a bit of a bump. The plane did work! From then on, many men were going to fly and go far.

God did help Orville and Wilbur to be the first men to help others fly.

Perhaps you will fly, also.